FESTIVALS AND **FAITHS**

EASTER

CATHERINE CHAMBERS

Evans

First published in this edition in 2010 by
Evans Brothers Limited
2A Portman Mansions
Chiltern Street
London W1U 6NR

British Library Cataloguing in Publication Data
Chambers, Catherine, 1954-
    Easter. -- (Festivals and faiths)
    1.Easter -- Juvenile literature
    I.Title II. Series
    394.2'667-dc22

ISBN 978 0 237 54121 7

Printed in China

ACKNOWLEDGEMENTS

Editor: Su Swallow
Design: TJ Graphics
Production: Jenny Mulvanny
Picture research: Victoria Brooker

For permission to reproduce copyright material,
the author and publishers gratefully acknowledge
the following:

Cover: (top) Trip/H Gariety, (bottom and back)
Thierry Dosogne/Image Bank
title page: Richard Passmore/Tony Stone
page 6 (top) Rohan/Tony Stone (bottom) Tony
Gervis/Robert Harding Picture Library **page 7**
(top) Circa Photo Library (bottom) John
Hatt/Hutchison Library **page 8** Trip/H Gariety
page 9 (top) Trip/ O Semenenko   (bottom)
Richard Passmore/Tony Stone **page 10** Anthony
King **page 11** (top) Robert Harding Picture
Library (bottom) Eric Lawrie/Hutchison Library
page 12 (left) Trip/ C Caffrey (right) Trip/J
Garrett **page 13** Circa Photo Library **page 14**
Travel Ink/Nick Battersby **page 15** (left) Trip/T
Bognar (right) Eric Lawrie/Hutchison Library
page 16 Circa Photo Library **page 17** (left)
Trip/M Lee (right) H Rogers/Trip **page 18** (left)
Anthony King (top right) Andzey
Zvoznikov/Hutchison Library **page 19** (top)
Tony Stone Images, USA (bottom) Robert
Harding Picture Library **page 20** Rosemary
Evans/Tony Stone **page 21** (top) Trip/A Gasson
(bottom) Trip/Viesti Collection **page 22** (top)
Trip/J Stanley (bottom) Trip/J Stanley **page 23**
Trip/ G Gunnarsson **page 24** Hutchison Library
page 25 (top right) Trip/G Gunnarsson (bottom)
Thierry Dosogne/Image Bank **page 26** (top)
Trip/Viesti Collection (bottom) Circa Photo
Library **page 27** Brad Markel/Gamma Liaison
Network (bottom) Jerome Tisne/Tony Stone
Images **page 28 and 29** Alan Towse

Contents

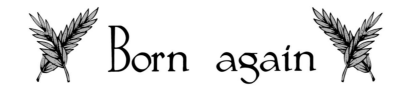

Born again

EASTER IS THE MOST IMPORTANT and joyful festival for Christians. It falls in the season of Spring – a time to celebrate new life.

The City of Jerusalem is where Jesus died and rose from the dead.

THE BEGINNING OF CHRISTIANITY

About 2000 years ago in Palestine, there lived a religious teacher called Jesus Christ. Christians believe that he was the Son of God. Easter celebrates the time when Jesus rose from the dead in Jerusalem, a city in Palestine. It joyfully celebrates renewed life. Christians believe that one day, they will rise from death, too. This makes Easter a festival of hope.

After Jesus rose from the dead, he gathered his followers around him. He prepared them to spread his teachings throughout the world. This is when the Christian religion really began.

WHEN DO WE CELEBRATE?

An important celebration was taking place in Jerusalem when Jesus rose from the dead. This was the Festival of Passover. It is celebrated by followers of the Jewish faith. So the first Christians added Easter to this ancient festival. Passover takes place in March or April. The time changes slightly each year.

A church in Greece is decorated for the Easter festival.

Some Christian churches celebrate Easter at a different time from others. Eastern Orthodox Christians come from parts of central and eastern Europe. They celebrate Easter later than other churches.

Christians hold services and customs throughout Holy Week. This week ends on Easter Sunday, when Jesus rose from the dead. There are sad celebrations in Holy Week. But there are glad ones, too!

Before the Easter festival began, other festivals were held at this time of year. From Iran, across North Africa and into Europe, people celebrated the newness of Spring. Some of the customs have survived to today. They fit in well with the Christian celebration of new life at Easter.

An Easter egg is the perfect gift for this priest.

In Guatemala, a brilliant Easter procession slowly moves along.

The Easter story

THIS IS A STORY that begins with Jesus Christ's suffering and death. But it ends with his triumph and rebirth at Easter.

FROM CARPENTER TO TEACHER

Jesus Christ was a carpenter from Palestine. He belonged to the Jewish faith. But Christians believe that Jesus was also the Son of God.

Jesus had come to Earth to teach people how to live better lives. But Jesus knew that his beliefs would make some people angry. He knew that in the end, these people would want him dead.

But Jesus carried on spreading his message of love for God and for all people on Earth. He also performed amazing miracles. Jesus gathered 12 faithful followers around him, known as the apostles. They became the earliest disciples – the first Christian teachers.

Christ appears to his disciples in this stained glass window of a church.

THE LAST DAYS

The last week of Christ's life was full of joy – then full of pain. Now famous, he rode one Sunday into Jerusalem. He was carried on a donkey – a symbol of peace. The crowds lined the streets, cheering and waving palms.

But by the following Thursday, his life was near its end. Some of the Jewish priests were angry with him. They persuaded the Roman rulers to arrest him. Worse, one of Christ's own apostles, Judas, showed the Roman soldiers where to find him.

Christ was tried, beaten and finally, on Friday, he was hung on a cross. His sad friends laid him in a tomb. They thought this was the end. But the next Sunday, one of his faithful women followers saw him near his empty tomb. Jesus then prepared his disciples to go out into the world and teach others. Finally, he joined God in heaven. Today, Holy Week reminds Christians of this story of long ago.

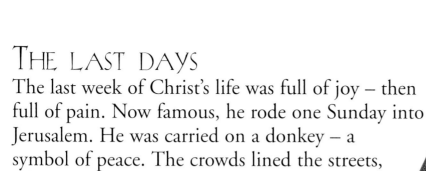

A Russian bronze icon with coloured enamels shows Christ dying on the cross.

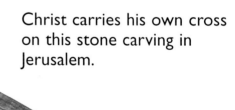

Christ carries his own cross on this stone carving in Jerusalem.

Processions of palms

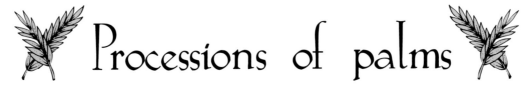

ON THE SUNDAY before Easter, crowds of people lined the streets of Jerusalem, waving palms and cheering. Jesus and his apostles were entering the city! That day is remembered as Palm Sunday.

WAVING PALMS

In those days, people waved palms when someone really important arrived. Jesus had become very famous. So the crowds waved palms as he rode into Jerusalem on a donkey.

Nowadays in many churches, huge dried palms, or pieces of palm, are blessed. This means they they are made holy. Priests and other members of the church then hold the palms up high.

The palms are paraded through the church. Sometimes they are waved in processions through the streets. You can see this especially in south and central America, and southern Europe.

WEARING PALMS

In many parts of the world, small pieces of dried palm are

On the morning of Palm Sunday, priests carry palms through the streets of a Spanish town.

◄ Colombia people are carrying a heavy statue of Christ in a long procession.

▼ There are palm fronds for everyone in Ecuador.

twisted and tied into the shape of a cross. They are then given out to all the people in church on Palm Sunday. Some people hold them, while others pin them to their clothes. In some churches, the palms are kept until the following February – the Christian season of Lent. This is the time Jesus spent in the desert, where he fought against evil. On the first day of Lent, Ash Wednesday, the old palms are burned. Palm ashes are drawn on people's foreheads in the shape of a cross.

In parts of Europe, such as France and Belgium, a small piece of boxwood used to be given out instead of palm. Some people fixed them above the doors of their houses to protect the home and the family from harm. Even the animals' stables had a piece of boxwood to keep them safe. In England, palm willow or the herb, rosemary, have been used.

Maundy Thursday

ON THE THURSDAY before he died, Jesus and his apostles were celebrating the Jewish Festival of Passover. At the feast, Jesus taught his followers ways of remembering him.

A WAY OF REMEMBERING

'Maundy' comes from a word in the old Latin language. It means 'command'. The Thursday before Easter is known as Maundy Thursday, or Holy Thursday. On this day, Jesus Christ ate and drank with his followers. The meal became known as the Last Supper, because Jesus died soon after. At the meal, he commanded his followers to do two simple things to remember him by.

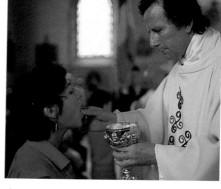

A priest gives Communion.

One of the ways of remembering him was to break bread and eat it. The bread represented Christ's body. The other way was to sip some wine, which stood for Christ's blood. Christians all over the world still remember Christ in these ways. They sip wine and take bread in services known as Mass, or Communion.

SERVING THE POOR

On this day, priests often wash the feet of churchgoers. This is because Christ washed the feet of

A Spanish lady from Seville wears her black mantilla on Maundy Thursday as a sign of mourning.

his apostles on that first Maundy Thursday. The tradition began in Europe over 1500 years ago. Then, popes, priests, kings and queens washed the feet of twelve or more poor men or beggars.

In England, instead of washing people's feet, kings and queens of England used to give Maundy money to the poor. Today, the Queen still gives out Maundy money.

The top painting from Romania shows the Last Supper. The bottom picture shows Christ washing the feet of his apostles.

 Good Friday

IT'S A DAY OF SADNESS for Christians as they remember how Jesus died on the cross. It's also a time for being sorry for things they've done wrong.

THE DARKEST DAY

After the Last Supper on Maundy Thursday, Jesus went to the Garden of Gethsemane in Jerusalem. Here, he prayed. But it was also here that one of Jesus' own apostles, Judas, turned against him. Judas showed Roman soldiers where to find Jesus. Jesus was arrested, tried, beaten and put to death on a cross.

This is the Garden of Gethsemane, where Jesus was arrested.

On this day, churches are stripped of all decoration. The altar is often left bare or covered with a black cloth. A simple cross, like the cross on which Christ died, is placed at the centre. The church lights are turned out and no candles flicker.

Bread and wine, the symbols of Christ, are sometimes left overnight on a special altar. The altar is guarded until the next day by a few members of the

church. This is to remember Christ's last night in the garden. Christ had asked his followers to keep him company throughout that night. But they just couldn't keep awake. The next day, Christ asked them, 'Could you not watch with me just one hour?'

Some Christians fast on this day. And in many churches, people sit very quietly between midday and three o'clock in the afternoon. It is believed that this is the time that Christ hung on the cross before he died.

Penitents carry wooden crosses through the streets of Seville, in Spain.

A heavy statue of Jesus is carried through a town in Ecuador.

PROCESSIONS OF PENITENTS

Penitents are people who are sorry for their sins. On Good Friday in Spain, penitents cover their faces with hoods and parade slowly along the streets. In southern and central America, they walk a long way carrying heavy wooden crosses or statues of the saints. As the sun sets in parts of Greece, funeral processions end this sad day.

Easter Eve

CHURCHES ARE DARK AND SILENT on Holy Saturday, the day after Good Friday. But towards late evening, they slowly light up, ready for joyful Easter Sunday.

CHRIST, THE LIGHT OF THE WORLD

It is Easter Saturday. Churches stay gloomy and empty until night time. In the churches of eastern Europe, everything starts to light up at the stroke of midnight. A flame is passed from one person to the other, so that candles and lamps can be lit. The whole church glows.

In Roman Catholic and some Anglican Churches, a huge, bright candle is carried through the church. It shows how Jesus Christ, the Light of the World, rose from the dead and drove away the darkness of evil.

The candle taken to the water is used to baptise Christians. Baptism is a ceremony that makes people members of the Christian Church. The candle blesses the waters for the year ahead. Hundreds of years ago, many people became baptised at Easter with this water.

An Easter candle standing in a gleaming holder shines beside a baptismal font.

FROM SADNESS TO HAPPINESS

People celebrate Easter Eve in many different ways. In Romanian churches, a picture of Jesus is laid flat on a table. This represents Christ lying in the tomb. The members of the church then crawl under the table. They hope to leave behind their sins as they rise at the other side of the table.

At midnight in Greece, fireworks explode in the streets as people shout, 'Christ is risen!'

An icon from the Lebanon shows Christ on the cross, watched by two women followers.

Fireworks mark the end of Easter Eve.

Christ is risen!

T HE CHURCH IS BRIGHT with flowers and light. It is time to be happy. For Jesus Christ is risen today!

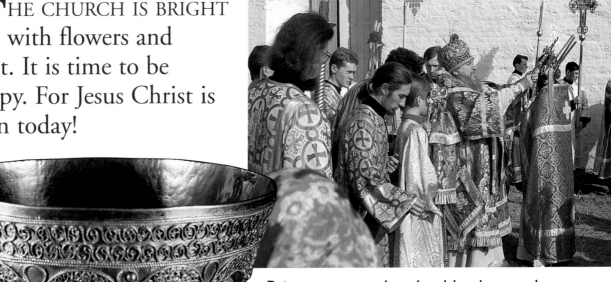

Priests wear red and gold robes at these joyful Easter celebrations in Russia.

OH, HAPPY DAY!

It is early on Easter Sunday morning as people open the church doors. What a difference they see now! There are masses of spring flowers all over the church. The altar is covered in coloured cloth and a cross rises from the centre. The priest wears his or her brightest robes.

Cheerful hymns are sung in the service. The priest gets ready to remember Jesus with bread and wine, just like Jesus' first followers. The bread is placed on the most precious plate and is blessed. A gold or silver chalice holds the wine. This is a really special day.

This rare golden chalice is 900 years old.

The Hollywood Bowl, an outdoor theatre in the USA, is the stage for an Easter service at sunrise.

SPREADING THE FAITH

Easter time really carries on for another fifty days. This is when Christ showed his first followers how to spread his teachings. Ascension Day falls during this time. It is the day when Christians believe Christ's spirit finally joined God in heaven.

On Easter Sunday, some services are held outside. In San Francisco, in the USA, thousands of people flock to Mount David, the highest hill in the city. Here, they hold services under the huge 3-metre-high cross that towers from the top.

Inside eastern European and some modern African churches, the churchgoers search for the body of Jesus Christ in a model of the tomb. When they find the tomb empty, they shout, 'Christ is risen!'

Flower decorations are prepared at the church for Easter celebrations.

Spring is here at last!

Easter time is also spring time. The trees are bursting with leaves and the sun is starting to sizzle. It's time to celebrate – with dancing, singing and . . . eggs!

Apple blossom and meadow flowers show that spring has arrived in Italy.

Wake up, world!

The ancient Greeks and Romans believed that the world woke up again in spring after its long winter sleep.

At this time of the year, people in northern Europe held a spring festival of singing and dancing. This was so that the gods would bring new life to the fields and trees. The name of the festival was Ostara. It is thought that we get the name Easter from this.

Spring Celebrations

Giving eggs is an ancient North African and European celebration of the new life of spring.

One of the first signs of spring is the shrill sound of birdsong. At the traditional E'maischen Fair in Luxembourg, china bird-flutes are sold to welcome the spring.

In the Czech Republic, girls chase boys and throw buckets of water over them – to get them bright and clean after the long winter! But they give them Easter eggs, too.

In Sweden, small girls dress up as witches and hand out Easter wishes for a few coins. Homes are decorated with twigs tipped with brightly-coloured chicken feathers in praise of the new spring.

One very old way of getting ready for the sunny times ahead was to sweep out the dust of winter. Nowadays, we call this hard work, 'spring'-cleaning!

Let's get clean! People throw water at each other as part of the Easter fun in Poland's capital city of Warsaw.

Dancers from Ukraine celebrate spring in traditional style – in France.

21

Festival fun today

IN MANY PARTS OF THE WORLD, Easter weekend is now holiday time – a time for fun! Games, music and dancing were once part of ancient Spring festivals, too.

MUSIC AND MOVEMENT

Music, dancing and parading are old ways of celebrating spring. But Easter parades are still popular, especially in America. The most exciting is probably along New York's Fifth Avenue. It's not an organised event. Thousands of families just take to the streets and stroll along in their best clothes. Amazing Easter bonnets decorate their heads!

In the pretty Austrian city of Salzburg, a modern Easter festival is held. It is a musical celebration. Since 1967, Easter weekend in Salzburg has been filled with concerts and operas. A lot of the music played was composed by the famous composer, Mozart, who was born in Salzburg.

On the Caribbean island of Barbados, the festivities mean lots of outdoor concerts and Shakespeare plays.

Bright Easter bonnets decorate a shop window in New York. Which do you like best?

EASTER RACES

In many parts of the world, Easter is the time for races of all sorts. Try the old custom of Easter-egg racing with your friends! You each hold a spoon and balance an egg on the end. Then you race to see who can reach the finish line – without dropping the egg!

On many islands of the Caribbean, fishermen, boatbuilders and sailors are proud of their crafts and skills. Easter week is the time to race boats from bay to bay around the islands. And on the island of Tobago, there are goat and crab races as well!

In Ireland and Britain, horse-racing lovers flock to the most important competitions of the year. But if you want something really different, you'd better go to Lapland's famous Easter festival. There, you can watch reindeer-racing.

A friendly tug-of-war between families is a traditional way of enjoying Easter in Cyprus.

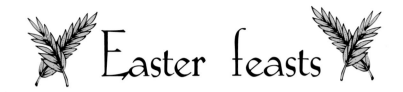 Easter feasts

YOU CAN'T HAVE EASTER WITHOUT SWEET TREATS, from rich, sticky cakes to Easter eggs!

SWEET AND STICKY

Easter cake in Greece tastes of oranges and almonds. A spicy orange sauce is poured over it. Russians eat pashka – a rich mixture of cream, soft cheese, dried fruit and orange peel.

In England, it wouldn't be Easter without hot cross buns! They're soft and sticky, with currants in them. But the most important part is the cross on the top. Since the Middle Ages, it has been a symbol of Christ's cross. That's why the buns are eaten on Good Friday. But in ancient times, before Christianity, the bun meant the moon. The cross divided the moon into its four quarters. Today, the buns are eaten for several weeks before Easter.

EASTER BUNNIES – HOW TASTY!

There are lots of newborn rabbits in spring. So, in parts of Europe, before Christianity, they were a spring symbol of good luck and new life. Later, people called them 'Easter rabbits'. Nowadays, you can buy chocolate rabbits to eat.

Easter bread in Greece is decorated with painted hardboiled eggs!

24

A Greek family in Cyprus tucks into a traditional lamb barbecue.

Lamb is a traditional Easter food. On the morning of Easter Sunday in Greece, a soup made of lamb's stomach, rice and lemon is eaten. The rest of the lamb is roasted for Sunday lunch.

Chocolate eggs for everyone!

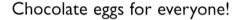

I NEARLY FORGOT – EASTER EGGS!

Easter eggs are decorated and you can play with them, too. But lots of people like to eat them. Some people peel off the patterned Easter egg shells and eat the hard-boiled egg inside. But I bet you like sweet eggs best. The first chocolate eggs were made about 100 years ago in Europe.

25

Bright and beautiful

P RETTY PATTERNED EGGS and spring flowers brighten the Easter festival in many parts of the world.

BURSTING WITH BLOOMS

Flowers have been a part of the spring and Easter festivals for hundreds of years. On the Greek island of Corfu, the flowers of spring are made into the shape of crosses. On Good Friday, after dark, they are carried in a long procession. The bands go with them, playing slow, sad music.

Nowadays in New York, there are spectacular flower displays in all the large shops. Macy's, New York's most famous store, has the best flower show of all. Easter lilies bloom in the garden of New York's Rockefeller Centre, too.

Flower festivals celebrate Easter in many parts of the world. At the festival in Avrig, Romania, women parade among the floats of flowers. They wear rich velvet costumes and tons of jewellery.

▲ Easter flowers in New York

EGG-MANIA!

Wooden eggs, ivory eggs, china eggs and glass eggs. They've all been decorated at Easter. Hens' eggs have the raw egg blown out through a tiny hole in the shell. Then the shells are painted with bright patterns.

Painted Easter eggs are to be hung up as decorations.

In Hungary, painted eggs are hung from the twigs of trees, like decorations on a Christmas tree.

In America, you can buy egg-painting kits. When your egg is finished, you can take it to the White House lawn in Washington. There, you can take part in egg-rolling competitions on the Great Lawn. Ancient egg-cracking competitions still take place – from Ireland in the west of Europe to Macedonia in the east. And there are always frustrating egg hunts!

An egg-rolling race is a serious matter outside the White House in Washington!

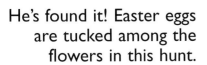

He's found it! Easter eggs are tucked among the flowers in this hunt.

Let's celebrate!

COME AND CELEBRATE EASTER! Try some egg-painting. Or make a spring-like Easter card.

MAKING PAINTED EGGS

You will need:
1 some fresh eggs
2 bright, thick paints and a paintbrush
3 decorations, such as sequins and sticky shapes
4 PVA glue

All you have to do is:
1 Ask an adult to boil the eggs hard and let them cool. Or you could ask an adult to blow the eggs. You just need to make small holes at each end of the egg. Blow all the egg out. Then let the shell dry.
2 Paint the eggs with bright patterns and colours. You will probably need to do more than one layer of paint to get rich colours.
3 Now you can stick some decorations on the eggs, too.

MAKING AN EASTER CARD

You will need:

1 coloured, shiny card - or you can paint white card

2 silver cooking foil

3 coloured, gummed paper - or you can colour white paper

4 felt-tip pens or paints

5 PVA glue

6 safe scissors

All you need to do is:

1 Fold a piece of coloured card and cut it out into a round or egg-shape.

2 Cut out a cross from some shiny or plain card. If the card is plain, cover it in silver foil. Then stick the cross on to the card.

3 Cut out flowers from the gummed paper. You could also use ordinary paper and colour it in yourself.

4 Stick the flowers on the cross.

29

Glossary

altar a special table placed in a church or other place of worship
apostles the first twelve followers of Christ who spread his teachings
celebrate to show that a certain day or event is special
ceremonies more solemn ways of celebrating a special day
fast to eat only certain foods, or nothing at all - often as part of a religious custom

mourning feeling sorry for someone's death
penitents people who are sorry for their sins
popes the leaders of the Roman Catholic church
processions lines of people slowly moving along
tradition a custom - a way of doing something passed down from parents
tried judged in a court of law

Index